AF429718

Hearing God

Learning to Hear and

Discern God's Voice

Kevin Young

Hearing God:
Learning to Hear and Discern God's Voice
by Kevin Young

ISBN – 979-8-218-45889-8

Cover image credit: Photo was taken by Kevin Young. This photo is an actual photo taken May 10, 2024 around 10:30 PM. There is no color correcting. Taken In Buckley, Washington.

Many thanks to Ericka Whitfield, and Carmel Young who helped with editing this book. Also – special thank you to my children who allowed me to edit this book while we were on vacation!

Contents

Introduction

For the past few years, there has been a hunger for God among the people of Valley Christian Center. This year, our expectation has been that everything we do is to impact the next generation.

One of the biggest changes we have experienced has been a desire to hear God's Voice. I did not sit down one day and say, "Let's write a book." I just started working on developing a lesson plan to teach how to Hear God. A week and a half later, this book was written. Editing it has been considerably longer!

My daughter experienced an evening where she heard God's Voice so clearly that she was awake until after 2 AM. When it came time to put a title on this book – I went to my 13-year-old!

She suggested, "Learning to Hear and Discern God's Voice."

I asked her, "Would you call it a 'Voice'?"

She replied, "Yes, but I would follow that with an explanation about it." She explained that it sounds like a voice in her head, and discerning is recognizing that God is speaking!

By the end of this book, my hope is that you will understand that there are many ways God can speak to us. We give God the Glory for what He is doing at Valley Christian Center!

Pastor Kevin Young

1

Hearing God

A while ago I met with a church member whom I asked to organize a group of people that have shown interest in praying for people. The request was to create a "Prayer and Prophetic Team."   We started planning, having confidence that we had heard God and had a direction and people in place. Our Church, Valley Christian Center, was becoming more than just a place to worship on Sunday! Revolutionary Worship (a monthly night of worship that includes multiple churches) is seeing people healed, filled with the Holy Spirit, and saved! We are creating relationships with churches across the state, and becoming the fulfillment of many dreams and prophetic words over us!

Not long after this meeting, we had a guest speaker come and he gave us some insight and direction. He sparked some interesting conversations. One of the things he recommended was to get a written plan for training.

After one of these conversations, I received a text from the original person I had spoken with. They let me know that they were no longer willing to teach this class. In that moment, I was so confused!

I went straight to prayer!!

As I prayed, I was reminded that our God is amazing and flexible and that it is possible that He can change everything in a moment.

I was also reminded that He will bring counsel to us when we need it.

I remembered hearing about Dr. Paul Yonggi Cho who led the world's largest church. As a teenager, I was told that it was a shame that they had so many services each weekend that they did not have room for "the Holy Spirit to move." I remember how this struck my heart. How can I judge a move of God that has attracted over 700,000 members as a bad thing, just because they were on a clock??

At the same time, I remembered hearing critiques about the Toronto Blessing, (A gathering in Canada that was known for the Glory of God impacting people in a multitude of ways that include healing, dancing, being slain in the spirit, prophecy, and visions. It was an extremely charismatic Christian Revival.

With the comment, "Barking and animal noises is not natural for humans, there is no order and it is all chaos," the whole movement was disregarded as questionable.

I struggled with these two extremes. One extreme is following a plan to the minute, and the other an apparent free for all with no plan at all.

Forty minutes after receiving the text, I had put together an eight-lesson plan.

To some, this may seem like an organized instruction plan, but to me, it is eight weeks of questions that I feel are the foundation of what I would want to learn about Hearing God.

When I presented to the church the idea of a mid-week class on "Hearing God," I was surprised and pleased with the response from many of our members.

There is an excitement at Valley Christian Center that I have never seen before! Maybe it is just me, maybe it is just a season. I have been watching what God is doing around the room and my prayer is that this is just the beginning.

But I cannot even start this book on "Hearing God" without first giving some testimonies about why this is so important to me!

2

My transformation as a Pastor

Covid was an interesting season for me. This was a season of one of the most incredible struggles I have ever fought. Honor is one of my core values. As an employee, I will honor my boss. As a guest at the restaurant, I will honor the server. As a member of the church, I will honor my pastor. As a citizen of a community, I will honor my civic leaders and mayor. The same goes for the governor and president. We have a saying at Valley Christian Center, "Honor Up, Honor Down, Honor All Around." We have been saying this for close to 14 years!

The Bible teaches that God sets the leaders in place – and sometimes He gives the people what they deserve. Therefore, elections are very hard because of the disrespect of radio stations, newspapers, and yes – preachers. I vote based on the platform that most closely aligns with my beliefs!! Unless you know the person, you can never trust the news to find out what they are like!

My dad was the mayor of Bonney Lake for eight years and there was one day that I came home from work with a newspaper in my hand and went to my dad and asked him, "Dad, didn't you tell me last night at dinner about (insert controversial topic here)?"

He replied that he did in fact tell me what happened at the meeting. I responded to him, "Then why does it say the exact opposite here in this newspaper??"

Oh, the pain, as he explained that the newspaper does not have to print the truth, they just have to say who they are quoting as a source. In this newspaper article, they indeed quoted a person and my dad was very familiar with the lies that this person was spreading. My dad just laughed and said that bad news sells papers.

Anyway, fast forward to 2020 and I had to decide if I would open our church against the will of our government. For me it was an easy answer – how can I teach people to honor, if I am not going to show honor now. Most every church I know of in Washington closed as requested.   As the time frame lingered on, the question became "when do we open?" This was not a problem for us, because the Governor said small groups could meet. We qualified as a small group so we opened with the first churches that were deciding to open.

There were plenty of arguments about God being the "Higher Authority."   However, let me ask this question, "How can I show the unsaved people around me that I love them, if I am willing to risk their health?" The unsaved people around me will never understand why we refuse to wear a mask, or refuse to distance from each other, or do not show honor for those over us. There was a very real risk, and nobody knew how bad the risk was, or was not.

I have an uncle that told his family, "I do not care if you have Covid, I want to come visit." Unfortunately, he was infected with Covid while visiting them.

He passed away about a month later.

How can I, as a pastor of a congregation that I love, want this for anyone???

Do not even get me started on how many churches I heard praying for a vaccine, just to hear the same people fight against it when it came out….

Then in June 2021, I came down with Covid. In fact, 3 out of 4 people that were at our church that weekend got it. Everyone had a different experience with it. Some did not even feel like they had a cold, yet tested positive. Some were sick a couple of days. One of our members experienced pneumonia, but never was hospitalized.

However, I ran a fever of 104 for 8 days. Only then deciding that I was so sick that I needed help- My wife says, "My husband changed mentally. He was acting different and it was too much to take care of the kids, myself, and Kevin."

We consulted a very close friend that worked at Good Samaritan Hospital, and on her day off, she met us at the emergency room door and she walked in with me, while my wife went home to continue nursing our children and herself as she was showing signs of Covid. That turned into 11 nights at the hospital, most of those days were in a "step down unit".

During the first week, I woke up to a room full of doctors and nurses. Prior to that day, there had never been more than two in my room at a time. My oxygen level was below 77, and they seemed happy that I woke up.

I learned later that at a blood oxygen level of 85, you start losing visual and cognitive abilities. I have friends that were put on ventilators at 79. I was never on a ventilator, but they did hook me up to high flow oxygen for a day.

One day as I was praying, I sensed God tell me, "That day was your turn around day, when I kept you from death."

During my stay, I talked to a lot of doctors, nurses, and nurses' aides. I listened one evening as an African nurse cried and told me about how her family was dying of Covid and she could not go home to help them. She talked about the injustice of the medical system in Africa and how you could not get help unless you knew someone important and had the money to pay in advance.

A respiratory technician told me, with pain in his voice, how he felt responsible for the death of a patient. The doctors did not understand what Covid was doing to the lungs and when they hooked this patient to the high flow oxygen, their lungs burst.

I asked the doctors, "How many people are coming in to the emergency room, after they are vaccinated?" Nightly a nurse would update me on how many major hospitals in our area were above maximum capacity (usually four or more.) She would explain to me that ambulances were being diverted to other areas.

We would talk about how few ICU beds are available at each hospital, and how the patients coming in are overwhelming the hospitals.

All this left me so confused, watching so many of my friends speak with conviction about how the church should be open, about how this was hurting our relationship with God, and you know the rest.

Through all this, I wondered…… If I was the Governor and all I knew was what the doctors were telling me, how would I govern??

How would I govern Seattle and King County? How would I explain this to "liberal" people, and what would I tell the "conservatives?" How would I balance the decisions of protecting people, and manage the damage done by shutting everything down?

Instead of anger and rage – I came home with empathy for "Those who rule over me!"

As our world changed –

As our church changed –

As I changed.

"Be kindly affectionate to one another with brotherly love, in honor giving preference to one another."

Romans 12:10 NKJV

3

Each Person has a Story

One evening, months after coming home from the hospital, I had been watching one of our family friends on Facebook as she ranted about the "Whole Covid Issue." She was very anti-vaccine, bold, and angry with the government. I decided to engage with her about it, and in a private message I asked about her story.

She explained that one of her family members died a week after getting the Covid Vaccine. My heart hurt for her – there will never be anything a doctor, scientist, pastor, friend, or governor can say that will change her mind. And if I try to have a conversation with anything but understanding – the conversation is over.

When I understand her story, I can grieve with her.

Each person has a story.

My 85-year-old friend had been inside his home for over a year. When I got out of the hospital he asked me about the vaccine. I told him what I tell everyone, "Talk to your doctor, do your research, and pray. After you do these three things, follow your peace. But do not take the vaccine out of fear." He proceeded to get the vaccine. The joy on his face when he told me about his next trip out of the house was so worth it!!

Each person has a story.

One of my mentors knew God was telling him to get vaccinated as soon as he was able. The DAY after his vaccination, he received an invitation to minister overseas, and the only reason he was able to go was because he had already vaccinated!

Each person has a story!

An elderly member of our church, took my advice and talked to her doctor. They looked at her history, health, and risk, and agreed that taking the vaccine would be more risk for her than benefit. She chose not to get the vaccine. She never will.

Each person has a story.

A church in Newcastle had the best presentation of the gospel with online services that were fun to watch. Then they set up a tent and started outdoor meetings. They honored their governmental authorities.   The Government demanded a list of attendees and contact information for each person.   This church said, "Absolutely Not." That is when the fight started. The church started getting threatening calls, attorneys' letters, and the church was on the news. I understand why they feel the way they do!! They paid the attorney bills and have the scars to prove it.

Each person has a story!

Through all this, with so many opinions, I kept asking, "How do we hear God??

Why does a pastor I respect feel so differently than I do???" I attended services in which they told us that we are not a Christian unless we fight for our freedom, and that every church must be open. These pastors and leaders compared the church in America to the Underground Church in China.

I had this nagging question, "Am I missing God?? Did my friends hear something different? Am I wrong?"

It had been over a year since I was in the hospital with Covid... and I was still recovering...

And then we went on a trip. It was a couple weeks on the road. We went to Universal Studios, Yosemite, Mammoth Lakes, and stopped in at "Fire and Glory" in San Diego. We had been watching Jeremy Nelson for several years and had heard great things about the revival they are leading. We specifically timed our vacation so that we could attend a Thursday night meeting!! We were excited.

Before the meeting, we stopped for dinner. The food was good, but the service was slow. I sent the whole family to the van while I waited for the bill. Because of this, we showed up at the exact time the service was supposed to start. To my surprise the parking lot was empty.

I went in alone to see if we were at the right place, and indeed we were! But there were only 5 or 6 people in the room that probably holds 400.

We went in and sat down, and the camera person went up and started praying.

The worship leader came up with his guitar and started singing. "Oh boy," I thought to myself, "This is going to be a long night."   However, the worship leader started "looping" and I had never seen that done before.

He would add different sounds to the loop adding to the complexity of the song. He even recorded his own voice and looped it so that it sounded like multiple people were leading worship. And the Holy Spirit was present. I looked down my row, and every one of my children had their hands raised, worshipping.

God was not done with me – When Andrew Hopkins got up to preach, it was as though God had tailor written that message for me. "What do you do when there is a battle?" he asked. Then he answered the question for me, "You don't engage, because God has already won that battle." He went on and absolutely rocked my world, because I was fighting a battle in my head that was so stifling – I was struggling with so many opinions. "How can anyone hear God?"

Later that evening, they had ministry time and prayed for people. After a while, Andrew looked out into the room and stated, "Where is that family? I want to pray for that family!!"   To my knowledge, we were the only family present. There were probably around 50 people at this time. We went forward, and God met us. The prophetic word came alive as Andrew spoke in such clear direction that it absolutely rocked my world. No one in that room knew what my son was studying in college, and yet Andrew started talking about computer coding.

He went on to tell my son that God had great plans for him and confirming that Nicholas was right in the middle of God's plan for his life.   He prayed over each of my children with the same specific clarity.

Then he prayed for me – he prophesied that I would take home the ministry, anointing, and fire that they had worked for 1554 nights to accomplish. He anointed us, in a way that only God can orchestrate. He had no idea that we have been doing worship nights or that we were leaders of our church. There is no way – but God knew. God knew that I want to be absolutely on fire for His ways and all that He would do in our church and city!

I came home with a renewed desire that the prophetic prayers would be specific. I came home with a desire that if there is only one family in our service, I want them to be impacted in a way that they will never forget what God has done for them! I came home with the realization that the battle is not to be engaged, for it is the Lord's Battle. I am here to draw people closer to God than they have ever been before.

But wait – there is more.

God started moving in our services. Our worship time started reaching two hours – which is rare for this church – for 38 years there has never been a two-hour worship service, at least that I can remember... Then we had a three-hour worship service, and someone's back was healed. When she was healed – I saw her face. The shock, the awe, and the testimony was incredible. We just had our breakthrough!

I have always wanted to be a miracle working church, a place that people will seek when they are sick because they have faith that God will heal them.

Soon after this, I went to Newcastle for their annual conference. It was a hard week as I struggled with the speakers and how they taught. The great speakers were just not my style, and spoke on subjects that I really do not want to deal with. I do not want to leave you with the wrong idea – these ministries presented a portion of our Christian belief that the world needs. Even if they can be scary for a nice little church!

Subjects like deliverance. It is one thing to believe we can be delivered, but to sit and listen to someone who is delivering people daily….. Or a speaker who has a passion for schools and kids. Her ministry is getting moms to pray. However, she presents it in a way that I was so glad my children were not in the room because her presentation was so graphic.   It was a hard week of self-reflection, pondering, and wondering. Was I here for a reason? Did I need to take note? Should I start preparing for a shift in our ministry? The conversations in the car as we drove back and forth from meetings was interesting as I bared my heart to my wife and sought the heart of God in this.

Meanwhile, my daughters had been watching some of the services on live-stream, and asking my wife questions that showed us they were interested and wanted to be in the room. They joined us for the last night.

The last night, Prophet Charlie Shamp started the service by telling everyone, "It is going to be a crazy night."

He continued, "There will be people who will have to be carried to their car after tonight's service!" I was excited because my daughters were with me!

Prophet Charlie chose this night to do an extended teaching and I was feeling bad that my two daughters decided to come that evening. We were in the second row. We were sitting right behind Pastor Darren's mom.

At the end of the evening, Prophet Charlie was ministering around the room and he returned to the pulpit and starts staring at me.

 My wife will tell you that he was not staring at me, he was feeling the anointing of the Holy Spirit – but I started laughing.   At first a chuckle, then louder, then a belly rolling, loud laugh. And I did not care who was around me. Then there came a point when I do not think I could have stopped laughing, but I really did not want too either. I remember praying, "Lord, if you are going to do this to me, please include my daughters."

I opened my eyes to find my youngest daughter, age 11 at the time, on the floor laughing. When I heard her laugh, I remember thinking to myself, "That is a fake laugh – I've never heard her laugh like that." Then I looked down the row at my other daughter, age 14, and she was laid back at almost 45 degrees with her head back and just laughing – again like I have never seen my kids laugh.

It was not long after this that Prophet Charlie proclaimed, "We need to run around this room."

I took my 11-year old's hand and said "Let's go." We did not go far before I realized that she was feeling the anointing of the Holy Spirit so heavy that she could not walk or run straight. That was the exact moment that I knew, beyond I knew, this is a God moment. This was not a natural gimmick just for fun. This was not just me being excited. This was a Holy Spirit baptism in joy that took the form of laughing – and literally I was experiencing the anointing of the Holy Spirit with my two girls.

We laughed for close to an hour that evening. There was one point that Prophet Charlie started praying, and I was literally yelling his words after him.

I have died a thousand natural deaths thinking about how I acted! It was not normal for me to act like this. I even considered writing an apology to Pastor Darrin, but then I watched the re-play online. The whole room was filled with people doing the same thing I was.

My spirit had come alive!!! In that moment, I wondered what is God doing???

Prophet Charlie Shamp had told us this would happen! I was not able to wrap my head around how anything in my life could change from just that evening. There was no prophetic word to me or my family, there was no special prayer, I cannot even tell you what he preached – but my family had an experience with God.

A very personal, life changing, vibrant experience with the King of Kings, Lord of Lords, and it was so good!!!

I knew while I was running around that building, that I want every person in my world to have the same experience!!

But the night did not end there.

Caitlin never left her seat. When it was time to leave – we had to carry her. Mom, on one side, and dad on the other. We stopped in the hallway to rest as Prophet Charlie and Apostle Darren walked by – looked at Caitlin and started laughing!!!

We laughed all the way home. Many times, Carmel wished she had driven. The next day, I went to work. When I got home, I went into the bedroom to change my clothes and started laughing – for probably 30 minutes.

All the while – wondering, "How do we hear God? How do we teach others to hear God?"

That night in Newcastle, I knew God had healed my lungs. Part of my story that I have not told you yet, is that since Covid, I could not laugh very long. I could not sleep very long. Life was kind of miserable. It was not like my world stopped – but I knew there was more that I was missing out on. And I think God needed me to know His touch in a very real, very intimate way.

I will never be the same. That laughing has become a confirmation that the Holy Spirit presence is filling a room.

My church has learned to just let me laugh!

One morning service the Holy Spirit laughter came on me so strong that I could not play a single note on the Bass Guitar during worship. We had kids dancing and then they started running around the room. As they did laps, I just stood there in wonder about how incredible our God really is.

Now, how do I teach those kids to Hear God?

4

Expectation

During the time between the decision to do a mid-week training about "Hearing God," and writing this book I had a fascinating revelation.   It happened as someone told me that during communion the week before, that person heard God tell them that they were not to get drunk ever again. "When you get drunk, you defile my sacrifice, my blood I shed for you."

Being drunk with alcohol is a temporary state of mind when a person does not have the ability to make wise decisions. Sometimes this leads to even worse circumstances due to the lack of self-control. Sometimes, people have consumed so much alcohol that they are dependent on it. The conversation prompted me to wonder why people want to be drunk with alcohol.

It also reminded me about my experience of the anointing of the Holy Spirit. Some charismatic Christians call it "drunk in the Spirit." This is a term that is used to describe an emotional experience, so overwhelming with the presence of God that the result is like being drunk. The long-term effects have led me to be incredibly bold about my faith in God. You could describe it as losing the fear of people's opinions causing a holy, or righteous boldness.

Have you ever listened to some people at work talk about going out on the town Friday night?

They plan all week long where they are going to go and what they are going to drink. The ladies worry about how they are going to be dressed, and the young men take showers and put on extra cologne. There is a sense of expectation!

Expectation that tonight will be a good night. Expectation that their fears will be gone for a while. Expectation that they will party and all the bad that happened will be forgotten. Expectation that no matter how bad their week, they can have a good time right now.

The reason that I am telling this story is that my revelation is quite similar. When was the last time you carried that amount of expectation to a church service, and were so excited about a worship experience that you dressed up for it? When was the last time that you sent out invitations to an event, and people showed up with an expectation for the supernatural?? I cannot believe that I have not carried this burden of expectation before. Have we gotten so lethargic that we have no excitement for the things of God??

Do you have an EXPECTATION that you can Hear God?

What happens when we set a culture of expectation and we start to focus our eyes on the Lord Almighty, with EXPECTATION that something good is about to happen? Where are the families that are so excited to get into God's presence that they clean up, dress up, and show up? One of the greatest miracles that I experienced during my laughing was that I literally felt like anything could happen.

I believe that our church is going to be a destination for worship. What God has done in me is so incredible that I know we can change the world. Can you dream with me for a minute?? What if the sick knew that they will go home healed? What if the broken hearted knew that there is a place that can heal that broken heart? What happens when the lost find their direction? I am trying to tell you that there should be an excitement that when you come to our service, there will be a power that is so strong that it will mark you, it will cause you to jump for joy, and to sing with a new passion.

You do not believe me? I should write a book just about the testimonies that I have been told about our location! This is an experience! It will draw you closer to God. It will also make you vocal about what God is doing!

It comes down to EXPECTATION.

What do we really expect to happen when we enter the room? I can tell you that there is going to be a powerful feeling. I had dinner with a couple who have recently been attending church. I listened to their testimonies about walking into the building and feeling chills as they climbed the stairs. This has happened multiple times to them. They **EXPECTED** God to be real to them.

At one of our Revolutionary Worship nights, I prayed for a young wife. Her husband was standing behind her. I could tell from his stance that he was a "Catcher." (Some meetings experience people falling when the "power of God" rests on them. Often someone will be trained to "Catch" them so they do not get hurt hitting the floor.)

This evening, the catcher fell to the floor first and then his wife went down too! When it is Holy Spirit, people can fall and not get hurt!

I must admit that some Holy Spirit inspired dreams were becoming evident when I need catchers for my catchers! There is a Power in the room and we need to wake up and **EXPECT** God's presence. The best part of that testimony is that several people from the group told me, "He never goes down, and he had been praying that God would touch him in this way!"

One of the Worship nights, I brought a pastor and his wife to the front and we prayed over them. It was a good evening and powerful prayer time.   Late that evening I received a text from the pastor and he thanked me for taking time to pray over him. "My wife just told me that she cannot remember the last time people prayed over us," he explained. He went on to tell me how much the evening meant to him, and how important it was!

A few months back, someone asked me, "If our Sunday worship is this powerful – what will happen on our next Revolutionary Worship night?"   This was such a great moment for me.   The expectation for the worship night just ratcheted up a whole bunch because our Sunday morning service is powerful.

I have wild and crazy dreams for our church!! I dream of people being healed. I dream of impacting people through prophetic revelation that connects them to the will of God in a very special, and very real way.

Why?? Because I have experienced this in my own life. I would love to have the freedom to travel the world and go to where the Glory is – except that I know that it would not make me happy.   What is going to make me happy is when the Glory is right here, in my home church – impacting the people around me.

The best part of my dream is that I am not doing the work! God is!! I have said since I was a young Pastor that I wanted to develop a team of ministers. I NEVER want people to stand in line and say only "he" can pray for me. I desire that there will be people in the room equally and better equipped for the work!!

But someone must go first.   Someone must lead. Someone must be the cheer leader and proclaim the good news.

Can we hear God?

Yes, but **there must be EXPECTATION!**

"This is why I wait upon you, expecting your breakthrough, for your Word brings me hope."
Psalms 130:5-6 TPT

5

Time with God – Bible Reading

In my quest to teach people how to "Hear God," HERE IS THE MAGIC SECRET: ***You must spend Time with God***.

I am going to present four steps about how you can spend time with God. If we are going to Hear God – we should start with the easiest form of listening possible.

In 1991, at the age of 21, I went to Canada with my dad to a conference. My dad was a member of the International Association of Ministers (IAM). They introduced me to the ministry called Presbytery. This is where several "Prophets" would pray over an individual or a couple. One of the days, they prayed over me. I would define the experience as prophetic, clear, and powerful.

That morning, they told me, so much about myself that I could not believe they did not personally know me. Up to that time, it was the most powerful experience I have had. They told me that I would inherit my dad's ministry. They said I was a "David" and that I would go through a season in which I felt like I was in a cave, but that I had a royal calling.   The experience was so powerful that the next year I read through the whole Bible, twice. I fell in love with the Word of God and could not get enough of it.

Step one of spending time with God is reading His Word (the Bible).

When we read the Scripture, we learn about our Creator, and how He thinks of us and how he plans for us. We learn right from wrong – as well as some of our responsibilities and freedoms.   We can learn from reading about some of the characters in the Bible, how they both honored God and disrespected God. In a day when everything seems to be confusing – I believe that we need to take time to decide what is important. If what you are hearing contradicts the written Word of God, The Bible, then we have missed it.

2 Timothy 3:16-17 "All Scripture is given by inspiration of God, and is profitable for doctrine, for reproof, for correction, for instruction in righteousness, 17 that the man of God may be complete, thoroughly equipped for every good work." NKJV

Hebrews 4:*12" For the word of God is living and powerful, and sharper than any two-edged sword, piercing even to the division of soul and spirit, and of joints and marrow, and is a discerner of the thoughts and intention of the heart." NKJV*

I think that the reality of what Hebrews 4:12 says is lost on most of today's self-proclaimed Christians. One of my favorite quotes growing up was, "Anyone can find a verse to support their pre-conceived idea." Many of us want to pick and choose our Scripture based on what we feel like. We want to feel good, not study hard.

We recently had a memory challenge at church that was designed to motivate our youth to memorize Scripture.

My wife and I talked and I told her that as a child, money was a major motivator for me. I encouraged her to do it.

We offered everyone ages 16 and younger $5 per 25 verses they learned. Then we offered the congregation the opportunity to give, resulting in each youth receiving $1 for each verse they memorized. When this challenge started, there were several kids who made it their purpose in life to memorize the shortest verses in the Bible. They spent a lot of time looking up those verses and memorizing them. To me, that is a win.

My 13-year-old daughter took the challenge to heart. She put in the time every evening to memorize. In two months, she memorized 166 verses

When my wife presented the memory challenge to the church – I felt God tell me that I was to give an extra $1 bonus for every Scripture that was quoted at our Anniversary Sunday. I showed up with 250 one-dollar bills for the bonus verses.

May 2, 2024, Talia quoted over 150 verses in front of the whole church. She may have preached a more effective sermon by quoting scripture than I ever have with weeks of preparation. She took home almost $320 in cash between the reward money and the bonus.

 I heard from three different parents that their children were talking about Talia on the way home from church and were inspired to continue memorizing Scripture.

One young man told his grandparents that he had already memorized more Scripture and they told him that they would continue paying him $1 for every verse he memorized.

Another young man quoted several new verses to his parents. Every adult in the room sat in awe of this display of memory work and was inspired to commit more time to reading and memorizing the Bible.

Four days later, Talia experienced the Voice of God in such a real way that she was up until 2 AM excited about what God just did for her. She was on an emotional high as she told her mom, and Carmel came and found me and told me to go talk to Talia. I knew something was up, from the look on Carmel's face.

After talking to Talia, I told her that she should write this experience down to remember for the rest of her life. I did not expect her to get a notebook and start at that very moment. Here is her story, in her words:

Today I asked my dad, "How do you know if you've heard from God?" Later in the day/tonight I went looking for a big Band-Aid for a scrape on my elbow. It was late and Mom was tired and getting ready for bed. So, I opened the cabinet door and started looking. After a few seconds a voice in my head said, "You won't find it there; stop looking." I kept looking. Then I felt like I was doing something wrong, so I stopped and grabbed the smaller Band-Aids and started piecing them together.

After I was about ¾ of the way done, I was realizing that piecing them together wasn't working very well. Then the voice in my head said, "Your mother is coming down." Seconds later I hear the door to the bathroom shut very loudly. The voice said, "Your mother is going to go to bed." Almost immediately she opened the kitchen door and said, "I'm going to bed." And as you might've been able to guess, by now I was very slightly freaked out wondering if this was God. I threw away the Band-Aid contraption thinking about how many Band-Aids I had wasted (4).

While I finished getting ready for bed I asked God, "If this is you, where can I find the big Band-Aids?" Then God replied something along the lines of "to the left most box in the left most corner." So, I went to the cabinet and found two boxes stacked on top of each other I asked God if the bottom box was the one He said, "Yes." So, I checked and it wasn't there. Then I moved the bottom box out of the way and there it was to the left of the cabinet in the leftmost corner.

Talia Young

A week later, I told Carmel that we needed to decide what to do about my bees. I am a bee keeper and have three honey bee hives this year. One of my hives suddenly had 8 queen cells – and I was talking to Carmel about making multiple hives. If we did this, we would not get any honey this year, however we would go into winter with a lot more bees. Or do we leave them alone and concentrate on a honey harvest.

Well, it was late – and everyone was in bed except for Carmel. Talia came into my room and tells me, "I think God is telling me that you are not supposed to do anything with the bees tomorrow." I answered her and said that maybe what God meant was that I was not supposed to make a total of 8 bee hives, but maybe a nuc with just a few of the bees. Talia responded with, "OK" and went back to her room. About 5 minutes later, she came back. "Dad, I really think that God is telling me that you are NOT to do anything with them at all." Wow!

The next morning, I told Carmel about the whole conversation and Carmel told me, "If we are going to teach our children to listen to God, then we have to listen to her and you do not get to touch the bees today."

I made other plans and had some meetings instead. Later that evening, Talia asked me if I had a good meeting and I told her that I was happy that I had the meeting and told her some of the great stuff that I learned. Then, I told her that the person I met asked me to thank her for giving me time to go to the meeting. Talia promptly told me, "Thank God, not me!"

I tell you these two stories, because I firmly believe that all of the time she spent in the Word of God is why she is so sensitive to the Voice of God today. Will you find anything in the Bible about Band-Aids and bees that pertains to me in 2024? Not likely, but the time memorizing the Scripture softened her heart and mind to hear God speaking!!

You see, there is no substitute for spending time with God and reading your Bible.

In Matthew 4, Jesus has gone to the wilderness to be tempted by the devil. Jesus had spent 40 days and nights fasting and communing with His Father. In verse four – Jesus answers the devil, "Man does not live by bread alone, but on every word that comes from the mouth of God."

Matthew 4:4 "But He answered and said, "It is written, 'Man shall not live by bread alone, but by every word that proceeds from the mouth of God.'" NKJV

I propose that the discerning of the Voice of God comes from your time reading the Scriptures. As we spend more time reading, our spirit awakens and we will be more sensitive to the Voice of God!!!

Reading the Bible will familiarize you with how God thinks, acts, and promises. When you spend time memorizing and studying – there is a spiritual reward that no scientist can explain.

6

Time with God – Prayer Time

The most common prayer today is one single word, "Help!" Many modern-day Christians do not know how to pray. We say we are too busy, there are too many things to distract us. Our day fills up and before we know it, we are headed to bed so tired that we cannot think straight.

Step two of spending time with God is praying.

I remember being taught that God loves to hear us tell Him the promises we find in the Bible. When I am praying for healing, I will quote from the Word of God about healing. When I pray from the Scripture, it builds my faith that there will be an answer to my prayer. It helps my earthly person to believe what my spiritual person is saying. Instead of praying my "hope" that I will be healed – I can pray in "FAITH" and believe that it will happen.

One of the amazing results of my transformation as a pastor, is that I walk in a new Supernatural Confidence. Yes, I still get nervous – and fail on some of the missions that God has put before me. However – when I am "in the room with the Holy Spirit" it is crazy how bold I have become.   I have been "Stubborn Praying" for healing. I will ask a person how they are feeling after I pray because I cannot see if the pain is gone. One Sunday morning, our Guitarist stopped playing a song and came to me. She wanted prayer for back and neck pain.

I prayed for her and I quoted Scripture to her. When I asked her how she was doing, she said it was the same. Instead of going back to our instruments, I prayed again. I had this stubborn moment where I was not going back to my instrument until we had our breakthrough. After the third time, she smiled and said the pain is gone. After the next song was over, I told everyone what had just happened and we started praying for the sick and hurting. Six more people were healed that morning.

There are a lot of reasons that I was so confident. For me, the best reason is in my Bible:

John 21:25 "There are also many other things that Jesus did which if they were written one by one, I suppose that even the world itself could not contain the books that would be written. Amen." NKJV

John 14:12-14 "Most assuredly, I say to you, he who believes in Me, the works that I do he will do also; and greater works than these he will do, because I go to My Father. 13 And whatever you ask in My name, that I will do, that the Father may be glorified in the Son. 14 If you ask anything in My name, I will do it". NKJV

Jesus prayed and people were healed. Jesus prayed for the sake of the people to understand that God is doing a miracle. I have told our church that since they did not take time to pray, they missed out on a miracle. God may have done an amazing healing. God may have done an amazing favor on someone's behalf or orchestrated an amazing relationship. BUT WE MISSED the testimony, because we never stopped and prayed for our request.

We often do not recognize that we just experienced a miracle, so we do not stop and give God the glory!

Last week my daughter lost the back to her earring. I went into her bedroom and prayed out loud that God would help us find it. We took her bed apart and looked between the sheets, and covers, and mattresses. I pulled her bed frame away from the wall and crawled under her bed. I was crazy confident that we were going to find that back. I told Cara, "God is going to help us find it." After all — we are in this crazy miracle season of confidence building. Well, after about half an hour, I got tired of looking and we stopped. I was disappointed! Two days later, my son, Nicholas found it on the floor out in the living room. WHAT???? My prayer was answered, but not in the way I thought it would be! I was blown away that God cares about a lost earring back. He answered that prayer when Nicholas was walking barefoot, and felt it on the floor. Prayer works — even when we have given up.

Prayer time is important to Hearing God.

If you do not take the time to pray to God — you are missing out on HIS answers. If you do not take the time to ask for anything in the name of Jesus, then you will not receive the best God has for you. If you do not take the time to recognize your needs, you will not recognize when God answers them.

Prayer Time is not only making requests and learning to recognize God in the answers — it is also a time for us to stop and listen for the Whisper of God.

Recently, I was studying and someone made the point that we hear God with our heart, not our ears. This just blew me away – I have been desiring to hear an audible voice with my ears. But this statement resonated with me. One of the phrases that I hate, and I think most of America hates it as well is, "Follow the Science." However, science does not promote that we can think and listen with our heart.

The Bible states:

Luke 6:45 *"A good man out of the good treasure of his heart brings forth good; and an evil man out of the evil treasure of his heart brings forth evil. For out of the abundance of the heart his mouth speaks."* NKJV

Mark 7:21-23 *"For from within, out of the heart of men, proceed evil thoughts, adulteries, fornications, murders, 22 thefts, covetousness, wickedness, deceit, lewdness, an evil eye, blasphemy, pride, foolishness. 23 All these evil things come from within and defile a man."* NKJV

Genesis 6:5 *"The Lord saw that the wickedness of man was great in the earth, and that every intention of the thoughts of his heart was only evil continually."* NKJV

After reading all these verses – I bet you are wondering, like me, how can we hear God with our heart? If the heart is so evil, how can we change. And that is the miracle of Salvation. When we pray the salvation prayer, we are asking God to replace our wicked heart. For example:

Psalm 51:10 *"Create in me a clean heart, O God, and renew a steadfast spirit within me".* NKJV

Acts 15:9 *"And made no distinction between us and them, purifying their hearts by faith."* NKJV

I am saying that Hearing God has become a heart thing! Before I was saved, my heart was evil, my heart was dirty, and I was living in sin. But when I asked God to save me – He made me a new creation and He gave me a new heart!

When I pray, it brings life to my heart.

When we are praying, we are spending time in His Presence. Prayer time should not be only when we are driving or walking. It can become a lifestyle, then we will change our world through prayer.

One thing I have dreamt about is pre-service prayer. We have a group that meets in a corner office at the church before service to pray together. They are taking time to be in His Presence before the service even starts. This has been going on longer than I have been the pastor. It has had an incredible impact on how this church has developed. For one, the people in the room have become closer to God and closer to each other. They have a friendship that has allowed them to pray with each other and pray for each other. They lift the church and the families because they are experiencing God's Love in a prayer time that is touching God's Heart. Many times, they do not know what they are praying for but being in God's Presence means that they are listening.

They are learning to hear God's Voice.

"Be anxious for nothing, but in everything by prayer and supplication, with thanksgiving, let your requests be made known to God; and the peace of God, which surpasses all understanding, will guard your hearts and minds through Christ Jesus."

Philippians 4:6-7 NKJV

7

Time with God – Attending Services

I must go here if I am going to teach people how to hear God's Voice.

Step 3 of spending time with God is attending services at your church.

Last week, my wife was telling me that during the previous Friday worship night, she was feeling God's Presence as a weight. I have learned that this is how my wife experiences God's Presence. It has happened to her often – and I used to find myself slightly jealous.

At our last worship night, we had a Pastor and his worship team from Edgewood leading worship. My wife told me that while most of the room was standing up front worshipping, she turned to our daughters and asked them, "Do you feel God's Presence? It is like a heavy weight on me, and I can hardly stand." Both of my daughters had to stop and think. Caitlin answered, "I have a tightness in my stomach." Talia answered, "I feel like I could lay down and go to sleep."

I am not quite sure how to answer my daughter who is going to sleep in the Presence of God. However, if these three had not been standing together in God's Presence, they would not have known how each of them responds to God's Presence. My daughters would never think that a tight stomach could indicate the same thing that was putting my other daughter to sleep.

In this teaching moment, I was so proud of my wife for taking time to invest in our daughters' future.

Being with people who are sensing God's presence and physically attending service are important principles for learning to Hear God. We do more than just encourage each other at church! The apostle Paul wrote:

Hebrews 10:24-25 *Discover creative ways to encourage others and to motivate them toward acts of compassion, doing beautiful works as expressions of love. 25 This is not the time to pull away and neglect meeting together, as some have formed the habit of doing. In fact, we should come together even more frequently, eager to encourage and urge each other onward as we anticipate that day dawning. TPT*

The Christian church in the United States has the sad attendance record of once every three weeks. Paul is recognizing the ugly fact that some are in the habit of not going to church, spending time with others of the same faith, or building relationship. This is the age-old challenge to attend a local church service weekly.

Seriously, one of the best ways to learn how to listen to the Voice of God is to be around people and talk about it. I learned to recognize God when others were praying exactly what I felt I was to pray. I learned to recognize a prophetic word by listening to what God was telling me and then listening to what others were saying in the same atmosphere. This does not happen on accident. This is not something that I could have done if I was not in the House of the Lord!

It may be embarrassing to ask the questions: "What does it feel like when God is present? What is it like to speak a word of encouragement? How do you become more confident when speaking out?

I know the fear of asking these "obvious" questions. I have been humbling myself in front of so many of my peers as I have been exploring the limitations of my faith. Yes, this fear places a boundary that says, "Do not learn this."

Let me encourage you. PLEASE START ASKING. Please start talking!! Get over your pride and admit that there is so much to learn.

Sometimes the fear of embarrassment is that if I ask a question, I will look dumb. Maybe I will even look like less than a Christian. However, asking these questions should bring a long-time, faith-believing Christian to joy! Every Christian will enjoy helping someone with their faith and helping them grow in their life with Christ. Start a conversation about God and what God is doing through them.

You will not have this conversation if you are sitting at home!

Jesus, in the book of John, is describing those who follow him as sheep that know His voice. Shepherds spend a lot of time with their sheep, and they do learn to recognize their shepherd from an early age.

John 10:27 "My own sheep will hear my voice and I know each one, and they will follow me." TPT

When you are His sheep, you will want to attend a gathering that loves God. The Shepherd will take care of the sheep! Sheep are social animals that run in a herd. They are not intended to run alone!

There are some legitimate reasons why people cannot go to service. Lack of transportation or physical disabilities are a couple of reasons. Sometimes our job will require weekends. In these cases, we must trust God to bring the right people into relationship with you to help you grow.

Oh, I know the world is full of Bible-believing, self-proclaimed Christians who skip church, and will not be around other Christians. But most of those people are staying home because of hurts that they experienced at church, not because they believe they are better because of it. If you have been hurt by your pastor and other people that say they are believers, please allow me to apologize for them to you.

I recently had an opportunity to apologize to someone with whom I had a lot of difficulty as a new pastor. We came to the unfortunate agreement that we were going in different directions. I ran into this person recently and I apologized to him, and then I brought him before my mentor, and introduced him. I apologized again.   I sincerely mean this. I am so sorry that they were offended and that it has kept them from fellowship.

My prayer for you is that you will recognize that corporate worship is a life-changer. Forgiveness will create the freedom to experience all that God has for you. Forgiveness will open ears to hear what God is saying!!

Another reason to attend church is that there is support. We think that we are strong enough to resist temptation alone. God did not design us to be alone. That is why He made Eve to help Adam!   One interesting fact about having people around is, "Those who teach learn the most." There is an amazing ability to learn when we stand and help each other.

Ecclesiastes 4:12 *"Though one may be overpowered by another, two can withstand him. And a threefold cord is not quickly broken." NKJV*

In a world of temptation and sin, we need to be in a service with other believers worshipping! In a daily routine at work, we will be tempted, tormented, and teased. We will hear jokes that are the gateway to hell. And a lot of times the path away from church is so subtle that we do not even think we are on it. First, we miss a service or two, then we start being sleepy, downtrodden people. We feel the guilt of missing and then we do not want to face our friends that were once our support team.   Remember the whole "evil is in the heart" conversation a few pages back?   Well, add skipping service and observe what happens to our heart!

Pray the prayer of forgiveness and get back to service!! Allow others to support you and help you to hear God's Voice!!

Please know that I feel for those who have made decisions that mean they have to work during church services. I would encourage you to look at your relationship with God and challenge yourself!

Maybe you are in a season, maybe you are going to have to work extra hard to make sure that you continue the relationships God intended you to have. Maybe you are being tested to see if money is more important to you than God? I personally do not believe that God intends you to be isolated!

I grew up in a farming community. When the harvest was ready – Church stopped! Jesus healed on the Sabbath, He walked through the fields and picked grain to eat on the Sabbath. There are a lot of occupations that require that you work during a service time. I am not casting judgment across everyone; I am asking you to evaluate yourself and your motives. Are you seeking God first? We will each be held accountable for our own decision!

"Until I come, be diligent in devouring the Word of God, be faithful in prayer, and in teaching the believers."

1 Timothy 4:13

8

Time with God – Your Environment?

Who is influencing you? What are you listening to? Who are your friends, entertainment, family, and church?

Step 4 of spending time with God is to consider your environment!

 At a men's group, one of the men was challenging the others with his testimony about listening to the radio. He was explaining to the men that he has found a new peace at work because he has started listening to a Christian Radio station and it has been helping him. He described the work environment, and challenges of working in a secular environment. He mentioned that he has found that worship music in the delivery vehicle is making a huge impact on his attitude.

Some people go to the gym.   Some people are so busy being entertained that they do not have time to study the Word of God and hear God. I even know some people who prioritize family over God. I am sure we all have friends that spend so much time together Saturday night that they are not able to get out of bed on Sunday morning to attend a service.

I also have friends that encourage me to attend service. I have a group of friends that are careful about their entertainment. They make sure that they are being led to the King of Kings and worship.

Work hard to keep your priorities in line with the Scripture. It is also very important to be careful about your source of news. Keep in mind that God is our source of joy, not the next news cycle.

I encourage you to evaluate how you spend your hours; not just your spare time hours, but all your hours. If you will be honest with me about how you spend your time, you will learn a lot about your priorities.

Some of the ways we spend Time with God:

> Bible Reading
> Prayer Time
> Attending Service
> Your Environment

This is a powerful list of how to spend your time with God. If you want to learn to hear God, adjust your priorities.

Please do not look at this and say, "There is no way I can do that." I recommend that you take baby steps. Start with a five-minute commitment! Start with Bible reading at the beginning of your day. Pick a few verses and meditate on them. Use an app on your phone to send you a verse of the day. Get an accountability partner; someone you trust to speak life to you, that will be honest with you.

In this season, I am so hungry for more of God, more of His Word, more of His Life-Giving Power!   I am encouraged when I see others around me desiring more of God too!

9

Decision Time

Now that you have learned how to spend time with God – It is time for you to confirm in your spirit that you can personally hear God.

It is decision time. It is time to decide if you are going to press into what God can reveal to you, or if you want to continue living life the way you have so far!

For those of us at Valley Christian Center, we are hungry to experience more of God. I was encouraged by how many people told me that they are interested in attending a class on Wednesday night for 8 lessons.   We are not able to meet every week, so we will be stretching this class over 4 months! I was disappointed to stretch this out so long, but the more this class developed, the more I realized that we need time to process what we have learned.

I want you to think about this decision before you make a commitment to finish this book.

Consider these questions and how you answer them:

Is God real enough for you to hear His Voice?

Is it possible for you to identify His promptings, with everything that is going on around you?

How will you decide if you are Hearing God or if you are hearing your own desires?

There is going to be some considerable spiritual push back because this will be a big part of your future. When you learn to Hear God, there will be spiritual forces that will try to lead you astray.

After you learn to Hear God's Voice you will carry a new responsibility. You will have to act on what you hear in a much bolder way.

Your first priority will be learning to confirm if what you are hearing is real.

Jesus said this about himself:

John 5:19 "So Jesus said, 'I speak to you the eternal truth. The Son is unable to do anything from himself or through his own initiative. I only do the works that I see the Father doing, for the Son does the same works as his Father.'" TPT

If Jesus can only do what he is seeing His Father do, we also need to hold to that standard!!! What is your relationship with God? Have you been spending time listening to His voice? Do you hang around people that can help you learn to listen? This is where the heavy lifting starts.

I believe that God wants you to have a close relationship to people that already hear His voice and can help you learn. But this means hanging out with these people, it means going to more than just a weekend service.

When I started hearing God's Voice, I was super nervous. I had to learn the signs my body would give me.

One time, I knew I was supposed to give a word to someone, and I was standing next to my wife and I put her hand on my wrist so she could feel my heart pumping. When I stepped forward and gave the word, the person confirmed the word immediately – so I had two confirmations for that word!

I went to a class on how to hear God. To start the meeting, the person leading the meeting told everyone that she was going to be seeing Pastor Bill Johnson the next week. She gave each of us a sheet of paper and gave us the opportunity to write him a "Thank You" note. I was very quick to take them up on that opportunity and I penned a note that was sincere and expressed my gratitude. After everyone was done, to my horror – the leader announced that the letter each of us had just written was a prophetic word over ourself, and now we get to stand up and read them to the group. I was absolutely embarrassed and wishing that I had not attended the meeting. The class had been promoted as a lesson in Hearing God, and I did not think it was very nice to start it out with this trickery –

She called on me to read my letter first. I stood up and read my thank you note – Telling "myself" that I was so thankful for the impact "I" have had on the churches as the result of my ministry. The care and love "I" have for the church outside my four walls was evident. The biggest result was connecting churches that otherwise never would have met each other. It was amazing to see people and pastors from many different church groups cross the isle and worship together, as a result of me.

Over the years, I have learned that the letter was exactly what God was telling me, not only confirmed over time, but confirmed by people in that room who affirmed the word immediately. What I thought was a silly exercise turned into an example of learning to listen to God.

One more story and I will move on – but this one happened just a few months ago. I was attending a big conference and there were around 500 people in the room. The speaker had met with his board in January and prayed over the year and they decided to take Scripture verses and print them on cards and insert the cards into envelopes. They printed hundreds, if not thousands, of verses and had them shuffled and there is no way to know who is going to get the Scripture verse. An envelope was given to each person in attendance at the conference. I opened the envelope with amazement as the words on the card jumped out at me and confirmed a prophetic word that I had penned the night before and was waiting for confirmation. My point here is that "Hearing God" can take many forms – but the most important thing I want you to learn is to confirm that word. If God means for you to get the message, He will confirm it.

The next priority you must make is to seek out your spiritual leaders. If your pastor is not a spiritual leader to you then you may need to find a new church, or change your relationships. This is not as obvious as that sentence will sound – for example, who does Pastor Kevin go to? Who is my spiritual leader?

I cannot change churches (and I seriously do not want to). There was a day that I had to decide if the church I was attending was where I was supposed to be! It was when I was very young and newly married. I was bored at church, and really wanted to experience something new. My wife and I prayed and consulted our spiritual leaders, and they asked us to wait until the end of the year. We never left. If we had left, I would not be doing what I do now, and our life would have taken a drastically different turn.

I have counseled several couples over the years that this is not the right church for them.

I will never forget a dinner with a couple and they tried to sneak into the conversation that they did not learn anything at our services. After stopping the conversation, I said, "I need to go back to something you said and make sure I heard you correct. Did you say that you have not learned anything at our church since you started coming here?" They replied that this is what they said, and then they tried to explain that I was not to worry about it, because they had several sources that they did learn from. What did the Holy Spirit prompt me to say? "Then you are at the wrong church – God wants you to attend somewhere that you can respect and learn from your pastor." To say they were surprised to hear me say that is an understatement. My responsibility as a pastor is to prompt a recognition of what the Holy Spirit is teaching, bringing Scripture to your memory, and teaching that will help you to follow God! Sometimes we need to align ourselves with the right people.

Some reading this will be wondering, am I supposed to change my church? This is NOT the case for most of us. Recently I had a conversation with someone who was questioning their church and my response to them was that the church they are attending is known for very good Scripture teaching. God will open your heart and speak to you. Most people will find that it is not their church that has a problem, it is your heart.

The decision is yours.   But now you are responsible for your attitude, responsible for what you learn, and responsible to Hear God for yourself!!

10

Why is the Holy Spirit so Important?

Jesus taught that He came to the earth to be a sacrifice for our sins and give us Salvation. Then Jesus said, "I go to my Father, and He will send you a helper." This Helper is the Holy Spirit. For the first time, everyone on Earth has access to the Holy Spirit.

In the first days of the early church, there was no written New Testament. I always understood this, but now that I am a Pastor, I often contemplate what it must have been like to be Timothy! "Hey world, you need Jesus!! He died on the cross for your sins, and rose again. Let me tell you about it!" But from what?? They had the Old Testament and it told them a Savior was coming. But they did not have anything in writing to confirm that Jesus was the Savior! This is why it is so important to understand the Holy Spirit!

John 14:26 AND John 15:26 say almost the same thing:

John 14:26 "But the Helper, the Holy Spirit, whom the Father will send in My name, He will teach you all things, and bring to your remembrance all things that I have said to you." NKJV

John 15:26 "But when the Helper comes, whom I shall send to you from the Father, the Spirit of truth who proceeds from the Father, He will testify of me." NKJV

Without the Holy Spirit, the truth of Jesus could have stopped being shared. How would the modern-day church even relate to Christ?

Every one of us must have a "moment in time" that solidifies our faith in God. This "moment" can be when we are so desperate we hit our knees praying. It could be at a summer camp when the worship was intense and we "felt like we were in God's presence." This "moment" could be when you were supernaturally healed. It might have been during the darkest time in your life, when you turned to prayer and told God, "If you will do (fill in the blank,) I will serve you all my days." This is when the Holy Spirit brings life to our relationship with God. For many of us, we can remember several "moments." The Holy Spirit will bring us before God, desiring His presence and impact in our life! We will desire to be closer to Him than ever before. If the Holy Spirit did not soften our heart to the Word of God then we would not recognize that we need a Savior. Many of us had this moment at the altar on our knees. This is what I am going to call our "moment" or "experience."

If we only have book learning and theory, it would be impossible for us to maintain our faith in God. When my belief is only because my parents taught me what to believe, I am at risk of losing my faith when someone does a better job of teaching a new belief. God has created us as emotional beings. He also created us intelligent, with the ability to judge, learn, and make up our own mind. He sent the Holy Spirit to direct us and help us discern truth from lies.

When was your "experience?" Can you still remember that time when your mind was made up?

The danger of determining our belief without the help of the Holy Spirit is that we could base our belief on an experience that is simply not of God. For example, a concert or movie creates emotions and plays with our feelings. Billions of dollars have been spent to figure out how you emotionally connect with what they are presenting. The emotional part of us wants to feel the movie. If they can get us to cry, laugh, and talk about the movie (or concert) then we will pay more money to go back, and bring friends with us!

An emotional moment, without the Holy Spirit, could completely deny the existence of God if we allow ourselves to believe it. This false sense of knowledge will replace the focal point of truth. I believe that is why so many young adults who grew up in a Christian home, get lost during college. They were taught from a young age about God, but when they went to college, they were subjected to lies that were spun so smoothly that they believed it. These young adults find an "experience" that is not of God and follow their feelings.

The Holy Spirit is here to help us see the Power of a loving God. What I am trying to say is:

1. We must have faith in God.

2. We must have Holy Spirit moments and experiences with God.

I believe that the Holy Spirit is here to help us with our faith in God, resulting in a deeper relationship with God.

 At Valley Christian Center, we work hard to make sure that you have ongoing moments that cement your relationship with God. We go to conferences, preach, teach Sunday School, facilitate youth trips, tell our testimonies and prophetic words of encouragement. We place a priority on worship that allows each person time with God. We are praying that you and your kids will have that "personal experience" that will cement your faith for life.

What about the sick? If we do not have the Holy Spirit and the gift of healing, how do we present the gospel in a way that is any different than a trip to the doctor? I have a friend that had a bad rock-climbing accident. He fell about 40 feet breaking both of his ankles, some vertebrae, and ribs. The pain was incredible. When mountain rescue arrived, they gave him a shot of opiates and within seconds the pain was gone. They were able to helicopter him to a hospital. How is my friend going to believe in a God that heals when he already knows the "experience" of the drugs? I have many other friends that have experienced the miracle of healing and it is only through the Holy Spirit that this can happen.

This generation is not going to believe a story, education, or training without a personal experience. They have been raised with movies, video, internet, and games. It has all been in such high definition that animation can look as real as a movie made with humans.

This next generation is going to need to experience something more powerful than technology to believe it is real. That is why the Holy Spirit is here.   The Holy Spirit will teach us and guide us into all truth.

At the same time, I have also watched this generation and the type of entertainment with which they are engaging. There is a lot of superstition, super hero, and magic in their entertainment.   Instead of being upset at this entertainment, we need to acknowledge that this is the open door for us to introduce God. They are seeking what the Holy Spirit can bring to life in them. They are seeking a relationship with God with signs and wonders.

In fact, Jesus said that He had not taught the disciples everything and that the Holy Spirit would continue to teach them.   The Holy Spirit is continuing to teach us today!

John 16:12-14 *"I still have many things to say to you, but you cannot bear them now. 13 However, when he, the Spirit of truth, has come, He will guide you into all the truth; for he will not speak on his own authority, but whatever He hears He will speak; and He will tell you things to come. 14 He will glorify Me, for He will take what is Mine and declare it to you."* NKJV

In my thoughts about the importance of the Holy Spirit, I would like to add that it is very common for some to point out that Paul told Timothy to "Take a little wine for your stomach." But Paul is also quoted in Ephesians with the following comparison – instead of being drunk with wine... be filled with the Holy Spirit!

Let me tell you this – being filled with the Holy Spirit can be a life changing event. Understanding how the Holy Spirit activates us is a lifelong event!!   I cannot put in words how much I desire our youth to seek a filling of the Holy Spirit instead of turning to alcohol for comfort!

Ephesians 5:18 *"And don't get drunk with wine, which is rebellion; instead be filled continually with the Holy Spirit." TPT*

Paul seriously just compared being filled with the Holy Spirit to being drunk. Two years ago, I am not even sure how I would have processed this. I have referred to my laughing experience as being drunk in the Spirit. Being "drunk" may give the wrong impression as we relate it to alcohol.

This moment was an amazing time with God when I realized there is so much more to what God can do for us. The result of this evening was that I feel "Power from on High."   I have been praying for the sick and seeing them healed. I have prayed for the lost and people have been saved. I am taking authority in the spirit world, with the power of the Holy Spirit.   The visible results of this "moment" are impacting people for the Gospel!

I pray that you have a Holy Spirit "moment." I pray that we have that "moment" often. I am praying that God will allow me the opportunity to be that person that facilitates YOU having your "experience" in such a way that you will never doubt that our God is real!

Maybe this book is your introduction to the reality of God working in your life, opening your mind to the idea that you can "experience" a fresh anointing of Joy that is contagious!!! If I am not the person that facilitates it, I am praying that you will soon be around someone who will!!

Jesus taught that the Holy Spirit is so important that it is un-forgivable to speak blasphemy against the Holy Spirit. In fact, this is the only un-forgivable sin. I have struggled with this definition my entire life and I have come to believe that the only way you can speak against the Holy Spirit is to have first experienced the Holy Spirit. I have been crushed to see some very popular evangelists "backslide." I have had church members tell me horror stories about previous preachers and leaders who sinned against God, separating their friends, families, and dividing churches. This is an example of someone speaking against the Holy Spirit. They have become reprobate.

Matthew 12:*32 "If anyone speaks evil of me, the Son of Man, he can be forgiven; but if anyone speaks against the Holy Spirit, it will never be forgiven, now or ever!" TPT*

Jesus also taught that the Holy Spirit will clothe you with Power from on High. When Jesus was teaching, He got their attention by healing someone. (Spiritual Gift of Healing) With the woman at the well, He got her attention by prophesying to her (He told her that she had many previous husbands and the one she was with was not a husband.) She converted the whole town with her testimony. (Spiritual Gift of Prophecy)

This is Holy Spirit Power from on High!!! Jesus started with their "moment" or "experience." After their experience, they received what He taught them. This is why the Holy Spirit is so important.

11

Are you filled with the Holy Spirit?

By now we understand that the Holy Spirit is the Helper that Jesus sent to us. As a result of the infilling of the Holy Spirit, we will do more and greater works than Jesus did! (Infilling is a term we use to describe when the Holy Spirit is invited into our heart!) We must accept the Sacrifice that Jesus paid for our sin to know that we are going to heaven, and the gift of the Holy Spirit is where the supernatural power is!

The Holy Spirit helps us hear God! The Holy Spirit brings recognition and validates what we are hearing. This recognition of the Holy Spirit is what makes us BOLD!

The Bible teaches us that Jesus was anointed with power and authority when the Holy Spirit descended from heaven like a Dove and landed on Him at His baptism. What if Jesus never did a miracle when He was growing up? The Bible does not tell us what His childhood was like. It is completely possible that He knew He was the Son of God, and did not operate in supernatural ways until after He was baptized and filled with the Holy Spirit. The Bible tells us He was full of wisdom and impressed the Priests. But there is nothing about supernatural miracles. In fact, the Gospel of John is very clear that His first miracle was turning water into wine.

This is one of the reasons I believe it is possible to be saved without being filled with the Holy Spirit.

To experience the real power of God, we need the Holy Spirit. Jesus said he only did what he saw the Father doing. This was made possible with the Holy Spirit.

The Holy Spirit is the enabler of all the spiritual gifts that God has given to us. 1 Corinthians 12 gives us a list that includes: serving, wisdom, knowledge, faith, healing, miracles, prophesy, discerning of spirits, different kinds of languages, and interpretation. Have you been experiencing the "Spiritual Gifts?" If we are filled with the Holy Spirit, then we should be seeing some of the above gifts working in our life. This is one of the reasons that we see people start serving at church. It is one of the easiest ways to start operating in our new found Holy Spirit gifts! I say it is the easiest way, but the truth is that serving is not easy for everyone. For some, they have the gift of Faith. They can believe the impossible, easier than they can serve. Others find that they have gifts that were not naturally there before!

At times, I must remind myself that I was already operating in the gifts of the Spirit prior to my experiences of laughing. But let me tell you that the Holy Ghost Power is real. When the Holy Spirit is working in me, I feel so confident that the Power of God is in the room. There are times when I feel like I am clothed in the Holy Spirit. It is different! It is not my power. It is all God, and it is amazing. It makes me want more! And when my cup is full, it runs over and splashes on those around me! And when everyone's cup is full and overflowing, we become like tributaries that join to become a creek, then multiple creeks join to become a River of the Power of God.

God is healing bodies and minds.   He is mending relationships with each other and with God. Restoring life! Helping us to hear God!

Luke 24:49 "I will send the fulfillment of the Father's promise to you, so stay here in the city until you are clothed with the mighty power of heaven" TPT

John 14:16-17 "And I will ask the Father and He will give you another Savior, the Holy Spirit of Truth, who will be to you a friend just like me – and he will never leave you. The world won't receive him because they can't see him or know him. But you know him intimately because he remains with you and will live inside you." TPT

Together, we have explored ways to know if you are filled with the Holy Spirit and Power from on High. This is not a common teaching in the churches of the United States, but I think you can see from the Bible that it should be!

I am excited to teach you this because it is my experience!! It is exciting to live with the power of God and seeing healings and miracles.

There is an easier way to confirm when you are filled with the Holy Spirit……   It is the evidence of speaking in tongues.

"But I promise you this – the Holy Spirit will come upon you, and you will be seized with power. You will be my messengers to Jerusalem, throughout Judea, the distant provinces – even to the remotest places on earth"

Acts 1:8 TPT

12

Holy Spirit – Speaking in Tongues

"Must we speak in tongues?"

That is a very revealing question. It is a question that comes from **(1)** a rebellious heart, **(2)** someone who is curious about it and has not experienced it, or **(3)** someone who does not know about speaking in tongues. There is a fourth person – **(4)** someone who isn't asking….

By rebellious, I am speaking to the argumentative person who just does not want to speak in tongues. I do not mean the heart that is sinning against God and going to hell. This question is revealing a heart that has not been fully committed to God – regardless of the cost.

Think about every **(1)** person that has argued that they do not need to speak in tongues…. I know, I wish I did not have to write this. But really, "I do not believe that I need to speak in tongues" is really code for "I have bitterness and unforgiveness in me and I really need help – I am just not ready for it yet."

I would challenge this person to do some soul searching and praying. Seek God in this area! Have you forgiven others in the same way God has forgiven you? Please know that Jesus loves you, and you are His favorite!   And He would love nothing more than to help you to break free of the bondage and chains of your past.

The second type is the **(2)** person that is learning about speaking in tongues, but has not experienced it yet. This person has been around others who have been speaking in tongues and maybe even watched the miracles that happen when the Holy Spirit is working! This person may still be trying to figure out what is fake and what is real. Unfortunately, what we as humans do not understand, we will classify as fake. But once you experience it, then you realize that there are some things that we will never understand.

The third type is the **(3)** person that has been saved, and just does not know about speaking in tongues! Yes, you are saved if you prayed the prayer of salvation! You are going to heaven, even without speaking in tongues. You will go to heaven even if you have not been baptized in water. But have you really lived? Have you experienced the joy of salvation to its fullest? Have you learned to pray? Are you seeing answers to your prayers?

The last person, **(4),** may believe that they do not need the evidence of speaking in tongues. They refer to the verse about "Speaking in Tongues" being a gift and explain that they just do not need to. They will even point to their good works, and sometimes amazing works. They also do not argue about this topic. They just let it go. If there is an argument, I believe it starts from the prompting of the Holy Spirit! I do not find any Biblical evidence that shows that we will not speak in tongues.

In those times that you do not know how to pray, or what to pray for, the Holy Spirit will pray through you.

I hope that you are interested in taking your salvation to a new level of involvement. There is more to hearing God than only listening to your pastor on Sunday. If you have read this far into this book – you must be curious and ready for your miracle breakthrough!   The Holy Spirit is causing you to be interested!

The apostle Paul makes it very clear that being saved, filled with the Holy Spirit with the evidence of speaking in tongues, and being baptized in water are all important.

Acts 2:4 "They were all filled and equipped with the Holy Spirit and were inspired to speak in tongues – empowered by the Spirit to speak in languages they had never learned!" TPT

Acts 10:44-46 "While Peter was speaking, the Holy Spirit cascaded over all those listening to his message. 45 The Jewish brothers who had accompanied Peter were astounded that the gift of the Holy Spirit was poured out on people who weren't Jews, 46 for they heard them speaking in supernaturally given languages and passionately praising God." TPT

Acts 19:6-7 "And when Paul laid his hands on each of the twelve, the Holy Spirit manifested and they immediately spoke in tongues and prophesied." TPT

*Mark 16:17 **"And these miracle signs will accompany those who believe: They will drive out demons in the power of my name. They will speak in tongues." TPT***

I think that Mark 16:17 says it the clearest – the signs that will accompany believers are casting out demons and speaking in tongues. Wow, that is a test right there. How many Christians are walking around casting out demons?

Maybe you want the gift of healing, gift of baptism, gift of teaching, or the gift of evangelizing. These are all good gifts, but they are not the sign of being saved.

According to Mark, the true sign of a believer is driving out demons and speaking in tongues...

I think at this point, a reminder that it is easier to speak in tongues than drive out demons would be in order! In Bible days, nobody told the new believers that they should speak in tongues. It just happened. There is no evidence that the apostles held prayer meetings with the purpose of helping people speak in tongues. In fact, all they did was lay hands on them and pray. They did not know what to expect in the upper room, as prior to that event, speaking in tongues was never mentioned before.

In our journey to hear God – speaking in tongues is going to be powerful. You are hearing the words before you say them. There is no pressure to understand them. We already know that we are not supposed to understand them. The Holy Spirit will be strengthening us to hear God through every prayer we speak.

I know someone who was praying in tongues for a while. He only knew two syllables. They were "ah" and "bah." This was his prayer language for a while. While he was praying, someone pointed out that he was saying "Abba." It was exciting to learn that "Abba" means "Father." It is not every person that gets to find out what they are saying, but when they do find out, it can be a "moment!"

A quick study of the Bible also refers to times when you should NOT be praying in tongues. Too often, the following verses are used to explain why someone would not want to speak in tongues.

1 Corinthians 14:2 *"When someone speaks in tongues, no one understands a word he says, because he's not speaking to people, but to God – he is speaking intimate mysteries in the Spirit."* TPT

1 Corinthians 14:13-14 *"So then, if you speak in a tongue, pray for the interpretation to be able to unfold the meaning of what you are saying. 14 For if I am praying in a tongue, my spirit is engaged in prayer but I have no clear understanding of what is being said."* TPT

1 Corinthians 14:15-17 *"So here's what I've concluded. I will pray in the Spirit, but I will also pray with my mind engaged. I will sing rapturous praises in the Spirit, but I will also sing with my mind engaged. 16 Otherwise, if you are praising God in your spirit, how could someone without the gift participate by adding his "amen" to your giving of thanks, since he doesn't have a clue of what you're saying? 17 Your praise to God is admirable, but it does nothing to strengthen and build up others."* TPT

In 1 Corinthians, The Apostle Paul was teaching a gathering of new Christians. They just found out what it is like to be excited about what God is doing in their world! They cannot wait to tell their friends. They did not have a New Testament Bible. This was even before they received letters from Paul. THINK ABOUT THAT!!!

I am talking about the first gatherings of people that we now call a church. We teach out of the New Testament a lot and I cannot image how they must have felt when they gathered.

Imagine if I had experienced laughing, the power of God, speaking in tongues, and had no Bible to reference anything!! Then suddenly we have thousands of people wanting to join with us and learn together!!

It was in this environment that the Apostle Paul wrote 1 Corinthians. He was teaching them to have an order to their service. He was dealing with so many excited new believers that he had to reign in the excitement and tell them "In each service, no more than three people can give a message in tongues" and "If you pray in tongues, pray for an interpretation!" It would be so easy for me to pray for our church to experience the laughing, every week!!! It would be a major party every time we get together! The Apostle Paul is teaching that we need to bring an element of discipline to the crazy miracles that happen in that environment!

13

Holy Spirit - Activation

By now, I am believing that you want the Holy Spirit in a brand new, deeper experience. How do we activate this in our life?

First, we must acknowledge that we desire to be filled with the Holy Spirit.

When we were saved, most of us raised our hand and walked to the front of a room. That takes a supernatural desire! Some of us prayed with our parents or a friend.

One of the results of our salvation is a desire for the Holy Spirit, with speaking in tongues. It is a gift and all we need to do is receive it.

I believe that Speaking in Tongues is one of the clearest ways to confirm our salvation! It is something we never did before we were saved!

Second, we must simply ask.

I will be the first to admit that if you are in a room surrounded with worshiping people, it will be easier. There is something special about "Atmosphere." I think that half the effort is over when we are in an environment of worship, with some music proclaiming that God is our good Father! For some people it is easier when they are alone. This way they are not under any pressure, and will not feel like others are watching them.

Third, we simply need to acknowledge that Jesus has already said it is done!

It will be important to pray out loud, or you will not know when you are speaking in tongues. Most of us will start by praying in our mind. To "speak" means to talk out loud.

This experience is different for each of us. What we do have in common is that it sounds funny, and unnatural. Remember that speaking in tongues is a language that you will not understand and the Holy Spirit and God will. We are learning to pray in the spirit! It is rare for someone who is new to this to speak in long and varied syllables. Most people I have been around when they were filled were saying only a sound or two. Once you experience this, you will continue to learn in your own prayer time!

For me – I was around 10 years old when I was first experienced speaking in tongues. I honestly thought it was fake. I feel awful even saying that. I was in a prayer line at church in Coulee City and it was a mid-week service. I do not remember anything else about the service. I just remember being scared, and not understanding that this is a gift from our Heavenly Father. It was only a few syllables, and I repeated them over and over. However, it was the start. I do not remember when the vocabulary grew, and that does not matter. What matters is that I wanted to be closer to God. When they told me that if I do not know how to pray, the Holy Spirit will pray for me, I wanted it. Was it embarrassing for me to say those syllables? Yes

Now, when I pray in tongues, there is POWER, PURPOSE, and CONFIDENCE! The Holy Spirit is praying through me and I am super charging what God has already said He would do. Praying in tongues is easier than praying in English. It is easier than bringing a request before God. It is a lot easier than speaking a prophetic word.

Praying in tongues breaks down the barriers that the devil will put up. There is clarity of purpose when we join forces with what God wants to do instead of telling God what we want to do!

It is time to activate the Power from on High! It is simple, and powerful. And once you activate this in your life, you just need to grow in confidence and let God develop it. Welcome to the Holy Spirit with evidence of speaking in tongues!!!

If you are ready to experience this, all you need to do is pray this prayer!

"Dear Heavenly Father – I want all that you have for me. I desire to know that you are real, and I want to be able to serve you with the confidence that only comes from experiencing what YOU have for me. I want to be BOLD! I receive the Gift of the Holy Spirit! I want to be FREE to follow you when you call on me. Thank you for showing your love to me, by sending me the Holy Spirit. Thank you for your gift of salvation and forgiving my sins. Thank you for this moment. I believe that you will open my mind and voice to speak freely all that the Holy Spirit inspires me to pray.

Thank you that you will help me to overcome my fear of fake! I will embrace the real, powerful, life-giving expression of speaking in tongues!"

Now continue to pray out loud. When you sense the unfamiliar words forming in your mind, just say them out loud! I will be praying with you. I am praying for you as I type these words.

I want to encourage you to not stop praying. If you do not experience speaking in tongues when you pray for the first time, do not stop asking.

I had a young man refuse to ask for the infilling of the Holy Spirit. After some questioning, his mom figured out that he was not asking because he had already asked once before! "Why should I ask again?" he asked.

I also had someone else tell me that she only received a couple sounds when she prayed. She went home and covered her head in a pillow and kept asking God to complete this work. She stayed there until she knew she was speaking fluently in tongues.

14

Prophecy

Some of the most important decisions in my life were confirmed by men and women of God that I regard as Prophets.

My confirmation that I was called to be a minister was in 1991, through Presbytery as mentioned at the beginning of this book. I had told my dad years earlier that I wanted to be a youth pastor.

In 2006, my wife and I were asked to meet with Prophet Mel Davis and he told us, "In five years, you will take over your Dad's church. Everything he is doing is for you to make this change." A year earlier, my dad told me that he was going to ask Mel Davis to help him find a replacement because he wanted to retire around our 25th Anniversary, I went home that night and cried as I told my wife, "That was supposed to be me."

In 2016, I had three specific prophetic words confirming that I was to leave my full-time employment, to work at the church – one of them from a known prophet who had no idea who I was. Again, I had been living in turmoil trying to decide when I was to quit my full-time job in printing.

Notice that I said "Confirmed?" I want to be clear that I believe the prophetic word is to confirm what you are already hearing in your heart. These prophetic words confirmed that I was "Hearing God."

One of my close friends and fellow Pastor has had to bear the brunt of my questions. I know his church had been teaching classes about learning to prophesy for a long time. I attended a series of his classes years ago when they had a different church name!   I have really had to battle this one. I asked him, "Why do you teach everyone that they can prophesy?"   I went even further in my questioning of him and explained that I know the people that go to my church, as well as his – and there are people in both groups that I would never want to speak over my life based on the fruit of their life!

To give you an idea how hard I pressed on this question over the years, He asked me, "Why are you interviewing that person? You do not even believe in prophesy?"   I examined my question and re-worded it to him again.

"Why do you have classes and teach your people that everyone can prophesy? My problem with the church of today is the trend to teach everyone that they can prophesy, and that they will not regard a prophetic word as special and impactful?"   His response impacted me– and I understood him this time.   He said, "We are teaching people that they can hear God for themselves."

I am sure that I will paraphrase from this point on, but he is correct – the church needs to learn to hear God as individuals.

Is "Hearing God" the same as Prophesy? No – I honestly think there is a difference. Can we live in relationship directly with God? Yes, in fact the Holy Spirit dwells in us and is always leading us to the Father.

Is "Hearing God" something we can do every day?
Absolutely – and sometimes we get confused in our conversations. For example, the Apostle Paul says the following:

1 Corinthians 14:5 "I wish you all spoke in tongues, but even more that you prophesied; for he who prophesies is greater than he who speaks with tongues, unless indeed he interprets, that the church may receive edification." NKJV

1 John 4:1 "Delightfully loved friends, don't trust every spirit, but carefully examine what they say to determine if they are of God, because many false prophets have mingled into the world." TPT

Acts 19:5-6 "When they heard this, they were baptized in the name of the Lord Jesus. 6 And when Paul had laid hands on them, the Holy Spirit came upon them, and they spoke with tongues and prophesied. NKJV

Hearing God – Let me define it this way: We can hear God in every instance of our life. As we learn to listen to what we call the "Voice of God" we can find ourselves questioning what we have heard. This is one reason we need to make sure that we have "heard" correctly. I understand that what I am "Hearing" needs to be confirmed by the Holy Spirit.

Prophecy – Let me define it this way: Prophecy is a confirming word. Prophecy is speaking into the future. It will bring excitement to your goals and purpose. A prophetic word is something we speak to others.

Some of the prophets in the Old Testament did not live to see the fulfillment of their word. Every prophetic word needs boldness to be said! When a prophetic word confirms what is already in your heart and mind, it brings the Life that only God can bring!!! It will turn up the excitement!!

1 Thessalonians 5:19-20 "Never restrain or put out the fire of the Holy Spirit. 20 And don't be one who scorns prophecies, 21 but be faithful to examine them by putting them to the test, and afterward hold tightly to what has proven to be right." TPT

At Valley Christian Center, we are pressing into Hearing God. It has been central to the joy that I have experienced and it will be central to how we serve God. I propose that "Hearing God" is the early stages of prophesy. When we learn to hear what God is saying to us, we can then speak a prophetic word of life to others. The Prophetic word must be edifying, agree with Scripture, be from someone who is bearing good fruit, and come true! Prophesy speaks to the future.

Hearing God is more of a life style as we become more and more sensitive in our daily decisions and prayer life.

One of the specific joys should be when we hear God, and it is confirmed through prophecy. The gift of Prophesy will be recognized in some people who have been active, tested, and speaking His Word. The Holy Spirit will give clarification about whom we should listen to! This person will live a lifestyle that exhibits incredible faith and boldness to speak out.

I teach that it is Biblical to never take a prophetic word at face value. I teach our church to test the prophetic word. Allow our emerging prophets to make mistakes as they learn, and do three things with every word given to you:

1. Test the word to see if it is true, depend on the Holy Spirit.

2. If a word does not resonate with you, put that word on a spiritual shelf and see if it is something to come in the future. But do not make decisions based on it. Remember that prophecy should be confirming what you are hearing from God.

3. If you believe the word to be wrong, be kind and dismiss it from your memory. If it was spoken by someone you know, have a gentle conversation with the one who spoke it, or talk to your pastor.

It bears repeating: _A Prophetic word should not come as a surprise – it should be a confirming word_. After all, there is One Holy Spirit and One Father.

Matthew 7:15 "Constantly be on your guard against phony prophets. They come disguised as lambs, appearing to be genuine, but on the inside they are like wild, ravenous wolves!" TPT

Matthew 24:24 "For there will be imposters falsely claiming to be God's 'Anointed One,' and false prophets will arise to perform miracle signs to lead astray, if possible, those God has chosen to be his." TPT

In the Old Testament, there is a school of prophets. This sets the precedent that a prophet can be trained! For many years, I thought that smaller churches, like the one I pastor, would have a strong tendency to migrate toward one of the five-fold ministry. I used to refer to my friend's church as a "Prophetic Church," and another one as the "Teaching Church," and another one as the "Evangelist Church." Yes, I would even refer to my own church as "Apostolic or Pastoral Church." I always felt that once we started doing the worship nights we fell into the "Apostolic" anointing because we were identifying ministries, and reaching out to our community. However, on Sunday we are a very "Pastoral" congregation.

But this has changed since we started associating with Apostle Mark Tubbs. His book, "*The Five Fingers of God*" really challenged me to not settle for labeling our churches – but to challenge our own people to start branching out and learning their gifting!

The biggest change in our church, is that we talk about the fivefold and identify the ministries. We honor people as they branch out instead of trying to make everyone the same! How we talk makes a huge impact on people.

I have had the privilege of watching other churches as they operate this way, and I get to sit down and listen to their challenges and rewards!

1- "Is Hearing God the same as Prophecy?"

I hope, by now, you understand that the Holy Spirit is helping each of us to hear God for oneself. Every decision we make, direction we take, and part of our day can be influenced by hearing God. Prophecy is when we hear God and speak to other people and impact their life for God.

2- "Is everyone a prophet that can hear God?"

If you are hearing God, you can become a prophet. The difference is going to be how you operate with the gifting. Can you be bold and share what God is telling you in public? Are you living a life that exemplifies Godly living? Are the foretelling words that you are giving being fulfilled? Do you understand the weight of what you are saying?

It is more about your life style and your commitment to God.   Are you being used to edify, motivate, and help others learn to hear from God? Are you ready to be judged by God at a higher standard, because you are representing God. Just because you tell someone what you heard from God, does not make you a prophet.

3- "If everyone can Hear God, then why do we need prophets??"

The purpose of a prophetic word is to confirm what we are hearing God say to us. There is a supernatural excitement when we get that confirmation. Someone prophesied over me a while ago. At first glance, the word was very simple. However, my spirit leapt with joy when I heard it being spoken. It was one of the first times I experienced that with a simple word. This person really encouraged me with a word that could have been taken as generic or obvious.

4- "How does a prophetic word from someone else help me to Hear God?"

You will experience some sincerely exciting times as you learn to hear God. In the hardest days, and biggest questions, you will be asking God for answers. I wish everyone could experience the joy of praying for a direction in your future, making that decision, and then having a prophetic word confirm your decision. But every learning process starts with a small question. Is this what God told me? Is this dream that I just had something that I should take seriously? Then when someone comes alongside you and confirms the word, you will both be excited!

15

Different kinds of Prophets

My wife and I had a conversation as I was getting ready to write this page. She has observed that when I prophesy on Sunday, I have a pattern. 1. God will identify someone and something they have been emotionally attached to. 2. Then I tell them that God has brought this up so that they know that God Loves them. 3. There will be an encouraging word helping them to move forward in their faith and life with God.

I had never noticed this before. My wife then called me a "Pastoral Prophet."   I was blown away by this observation. We went on to discuss other different types of prophets –

We discussed someone who is a real fire starter (in a great way) and the type of prophet that she is. She is a warrior prophet because she sees the battle and does warfare against it in the Spirit. She would come to the person I spoke to and light a fire under their heart and send them to battle. Remember, a prophet should be confirming what God has already spoken – so imagine the surprise when the warrior comes and announces what is going on and they leave ready to fight!

There is the weeping prophet. This person struggles to get past the pain, the agony, and grief so that the person can move on. This person will find themselves to be compassionate and caring.

They ache inside for the person they are ministering to and struggle to help them to get better because they are right there in the grief with them. However, they need to challenge themselves and start encouraging this person to fight the battle and join the Lord's side and Win!!   I watched someone like this at church – from my point of view, they did not help the person – but, in fact, they did because they were following the Lord's leading, when I had missed it.

We have had apostolic prophets in the house and boy can they stir things up.   Sometimes it is wonderful – when they find everything in order and they are just reassuring. Other times they can feel like a bull in a China store because we are setting off all their internal alarms.

Someone told me recently that Graham Cooke teaches that there are over forty types of prophets. Since I am not wanting to write a novel, I must focus back on my original intent for this book – Hearing God.

Graham Cook said recently, "The role of a prophet is not to prophesy, but to teach people to hear for themselves." He was basically saying the same thing I said earlier that a prophetic word should be confirming what you have already heard. Does that mean that everyone that hears for themselves is a prophet –

In my opinion, No.

So how does a prophet help us learn to hear God? If we have a prophet speak into our life, and they confirm what we think we are hearing – that will help us to recognize the Voice of God.

The impact at Fire and Glory was so dynamic that I want it for every person to whom I minister!! My heart's desire is that each of us will become so in Love with God that we have fun "Hearing God." Then we super charge that joy when we "salt" that word with a prophetic amplification and confirmation!

When we are learning to hear God, we need to discern what is God and what is other voices.

"Constantly be on your guard against phony prophets. They come disguised as lambs, appearing to be genuine, but on the inside they are like wild, ravenous wolves!

Mathew 7:15

16

Different Ways God will Speak to Us

In a book about learning to hear God's voice, I would be mistaken not to try to list some of the major ways we Hear God.

The Still Small Voice

The most well-known way is "That still small voice." Some people call it conscience. Some people call it a thought in their head.

I was thinking about a Biblical example of this, which got me to wondering how many times in the Bible it says, "God spoke to…..". Was it really an audible voice, or maybe one of the ways in this chapter? That is why it is hard to explain the supernatural to an unbelieving person. They have heard Christians talk, and they determine that they will not believe until they experience exactly what they heard.

Emotions

Have you ever felt something and then been overwhelmed with emotions? Crying, laughing, excitement, and an emotional desire to do something?

We need to be alert to our "Spirit Senses."

The Audible Voice

There are times when God speaks audibly – like someone is in the room with you.

My dad, in the early days of ministry heard the Audible Voice of God. He tells the story and he can remember the exact stretch of highway, and he can tell you the exact words. It left that kind of impression on him. He told me that he has never heard the Audible Voice again, but once you hear it – there is no forgetting it.

Paul heard the Audible Voice of God on the road to Damascus and everyone around him heard Thunder. But when he got up from the ground, he was blind!

Dreams and Visions

Dreams while we sleep are quite a clear way for God to speak to us, I had one last week that was so clear, I never went back to sleep. I am excited about how God is going to use this dream to encourage Valley Christian Center. I told the church about this dream the following Sunday and let them know that we are to expect some amazing services ahead. This is the very first dream that I have ever recognized God speaking to me. I asked God to confirm if it was Him, and Bam! He gave me the confirmation.

Visions are dreams that we have while we are awake. I have been told that some people see them like they are looking at a movie screen. I have had others tell me that they are like thoughts in their head. My point is that they happen!! We need to be paying attention when they do!

Sense His Presence

Many of the people I know that have Heard God's voice is through sensing His presence – especially during a season of changes.

Usually, it is an uncommon peace in a time of trial and pain. I pray for this a LOT, that there will be a supernatural peace that only God can give.

Physical reaction to his prompting

In my journey, physical things like increased heart rate have been a major learning assist. My wife has arrived at a point that she can look at me and tell if I am struggling with a Word that I am supposed to give. My physical reaction includes a racing heartbeat! One time, I was supposed to give a prophetic word to a guest speaker and I told my wife, "Feel this" as I gave her my wrist for her to check my heartbeat! It was racing.

Some common physical reactions are: Crying, goosebumps, heavy weight making it hard to stand and a knot in your tummy.   God made us, and He made us to be sensitive to HIM!

Prophetic word from someone else

This is the easiest way for us to learn, because it involves someone else talking to us! It is in this list because it is a big part of this list!

Being Slain in the Spirit

Or as some of my friends call it, "A Glory Fall"

This idea scares some and excites others. The bottom line, it is something incredible to see people being impacted by the Power of God in a way that will impact them forever! I must admit that I want to see God work so powerfully that when we pray, people cannot stand. But we must be willing to let God move this way.

We had a young lady at Valley Christian Center who was being prayed for and spent some time on the floor. I asked her what it was like. She told me, "When they started praying for me, I felt like I was being lifted off the floor. The next moment, I opened my eyes and I was lying flat on my back." That moment was five or more minutes.

My daughter also experienced this. When I asked her about it, she told me "I knew when I was falling over, but while I was on the floor, I could not move my arms or legs. When I tried to get up, I could not." She laid there for over 40 minutes. She had no idea it had been that long!

Neither young lady could put in words what God was doing – but I can tell you that my daughter has changed for the better (I know that many of you thought there was no way she could be any better!!)

But let me tell you about another experience my dad had – He was put on the floor for an extended period while I waited for him that night. He told me, "It was like God pulled His chair up beside me and told me my life plan going forward." He never told me what that plan was.

Reading your Bible

Pick a time of day that works for you to be consistent. Most personal trainers will try to convince you that first thing in the morning is your best thing in the morning. But this does not work for everyone! But do not become like the gym memberships that get bought in December, used for a month, and then fail to be used.

Lunch with a friend

One of the strongest ways to learn to Hear God is to find a friend that you can compare notes with. This person needs to be someone that will be in your life for a long time – because you are going to be investing emotional equity with them.

I am blessed to have a wife that has learned when I am hearing a Word for someone in the room. I cannot count the number of times she will lean over and tell me to just go share it.

Angels

Hebrews 13:1-2 *Let brotherly love continue. Do not forget to entertain strangers, for by so doing some have unwittingly entertained angels.*

In any Audible experience, we can argue that it was God's Voice, or the voice of an Angel. I would be more concerned about the accuracy of what you are hearing than the particulars of how it was delivered.

Prayer Time

This one should be first in line. Our personal time in communion with our Heavenly Father, is the single most important part of learning to hear God.

Your Spouse

God says that man should not be alone, so He made him a help mate. I would be absolutely lost without my wife. She brings a part of ministry that would never be here if she was not.   If you are not married, pray for the right one!   If you are married, pray that God will continue to work in your partner to assist you, and that He will work in you to assist your partner!!

Your Children

Someone once told me that nobody learns more than the teacher in any subject. Once you start training your children you are going to find the holes in your theology, and everyday knowledge.

There is no greater JOY than watching your children grow in the knowledge of God, learning to Hear God!

17

Reaching the next Generation

At Valley Christian Center, we are so focused on the next generation that I have strategically planned and studied around their growth and involvement in all that we do. We have a worship team that probably has an average age of 16. Two of our current team started at 10 and 11, both on drums. Our lead vocal started singing at 13. Please do not tell her that we call her our "lead vocal!" All the activities that we do are tailored around the kids and youth.

I believe that the next generation is going to be a "Show Me" generation. I do not think that they will take our word for anything. This generation can put a box over their eyes, and be a warrior with a light saber. This generation can experience life-like games that have absolutely NO reality in the room they are in. In fact, I wore this box and took a roller coaster ride that left me ready to throw up. I was in awe of how it impacted me. The next generation has information at their fingertip – oh, never mind – they can talk to their watch and get the information in an audible voice….. "hey Siri" – "hey Alexa"

How do we impact the next generation?? Show them the Power of the Gospel. Stop watering down the reality of who Jesus is, and let these young men and women have a real-life experience.

Recently, I took several families to a service and the speaker was someone who does deliverance. He has a ministry of casting out demons.   As he was preaching, someone in the room threw up. A little later, a second person threw up. I watched as ushers started cleaning up the mess, as they were prepared with white buckets. I realized that this was the manifestation of demonic activity and this speaker expected it. Let me tell you – I struggled with this meeting. I told a couple of people and their response was, "Why did he let it happen? He has authority over it and should just cast them out!"

Well, that was a tormenting thought, and I pondered it for a while. But I came to this conclusion – I watched the young people that I had with me in the room and I watched how they responded. If the devil thought he was scaring these young people with this display, then the devil is wrong.   What happened that night was demonstration of the Power of God. This is a group of young people that need to see the Power in person. They would not believe just the spoken word.

For example – If the speaker had said a prayer, and every demon in the room quietly left and then the speaker said, "Every demon in the room is now gone!" Not a single youth with me would believe that there were demons to start with. These kids are a different generation. Here is my problem – I am guilty of being like the youth I brought. I have natural doubts that those people would be subject to demonic oppression. They are in church and we carry the Power of a Holy God!! So why was this even possible? Maybe this will be the topic of my next book.

For this next generation, they need to experience God's Voice for themselves. They want to hear, feel, touch, and see the Power of God in a real and dynamic way.

They want to ask questions and see the answers. They NEED to have a personal experience. They do not want fake —

This generation would never settle for the days of old when the priest was the only one that could do the miracles or read the scripture. They want it to be personal. They want it to be real. They want God.

What they do not want is a watered down, fake, wait until you are older religion. These kids are growing up fast! They understand way more than you think they do and they are giving us a chance to get this right.

My prayer for this next generation is that you will learn to Hear God's Voice in a real and dynamic way. Push into what God wants, and Live Out Loud!

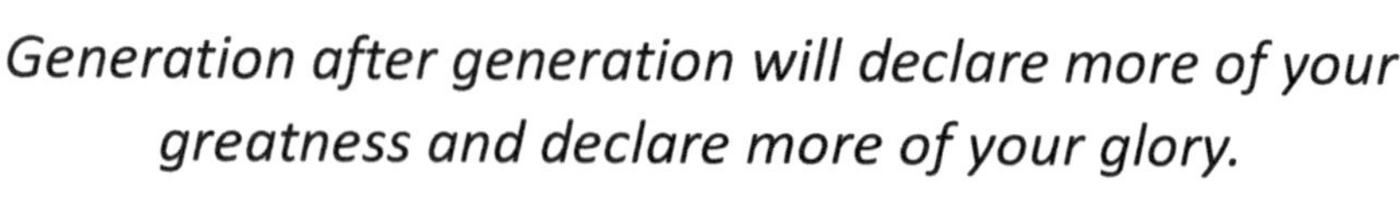

Generation after generation will declare more of your greatness and declare more of your glory.

Psalms 145:4 TPT

18

In Closing

I know this book sounds like I am over simplifying "Hearing God." This is exactly what I am trying to do! When we pay attention, the Creator of the universe is trying to get our attention and communicate with us.

What I cannot oversimplify – is our ability to Hear and Discern the Voice of God.

God spoke to Moses through a burning bush. He used Daniel to interpret Nebuchadnezzar's dream. He used a finger to write on a wall so King Belshazzar would read it. He spoke to Balaam with a donkey. He led the children of Israel with a cloud by day and a fire by night. He used a big fish to get Jonah's attention. God spoke to Mary and Joseph through an Angel. God is creative and loves us more than we can ever understand.

These Bible stories sound amazing, but the greater miracle is that we have the Holy Spirit and we should be paying attention to all the ways that God will be speaking to us.

Instead of getting mad at that flat tire, say a quick prayer of "Thanks" that you were not in the accident that might have happened if you been on time (think Balaam's donkey as transportation). God is saying He Loves You. Yes, I am saying that if you are paying attention, even the flat tire could be God.

We need to start listening to the Voice of God with greater reverence - and recognize the Power that God has given each of us, all the time!

I am this crazy pastor that believes that God is speaking!! Are you listening?

Is it as simple as it sounds? Yes, it can be – or it can be as complicated as you make it. Often making it impossible.

Let me add another thought in closing - In our walk with Christ, and our desire to Hear God, when we recognize His Voice – we are responsible to act on it. If God shows you sin in your life, you are responsible to pray a prayer for forgiveness, and change your life patterns to stop doing that sin. If He shows you that you have hurt someone, you are responsible to make restitution as fast as possible. There are blessings coming to us as we listen to His Voice and act on it. Why would God be calling us His Bride – and trying to talk to us, if we just ignore that conviction?

Too many Christians are going around making rules for others. Let us stop judging others and live by one rule!

I will love God with all my heart, soul, and mind. And because I Love God, I will recognize His Voice and discern what He is saying.

And that is how you will find true happiness – by desiring to bring God the Glory!

This book has been written to recognize what God has been doing and give HIM all the Glory!!

19

In Closing - Two

Hey, I am a Pastor! Don't I get three closings before the final AMEN??

I am praying for you to Hear and Discern God's Voice every day! This book was a lot of fun to write, and it happened fast.   This could not have happened if our Heavenly Father did not want YOU to read this story!

What is the Holy Spirit making possible in your life today??   I would love for you to tell a friend and show them the JOY that only God can give!

After experiencing this last year and a half, I am so excited just to let people know what God has done and how it has impacted me and my wife, but I am even more excited to tell you about what God is doing in our children and in our church!   It really is a LOVING GOD that can do all this and more!

And the Bible says He is NO respecter of persons – which means He is excited to do even more for you!!!

Feel free to contact me at PastorKevin.VCC@gmail.com. I would love to hear your testimony and answer questions.

www.ingramcontent.com/pod-product-compliance
Lightning Source LLC
Chambersburg PA
CBHW040151160726
48006CB00014B/1700